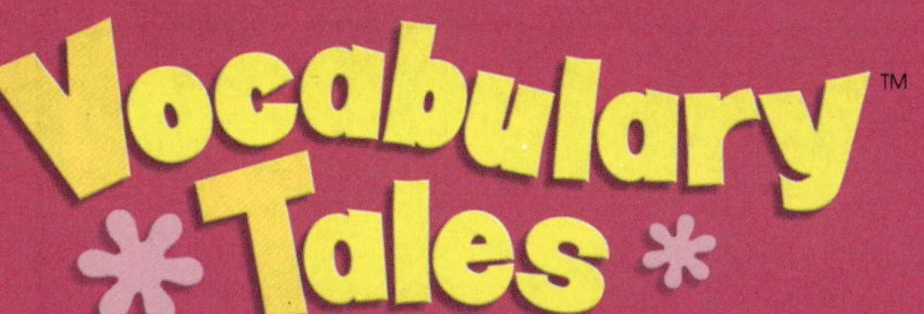

Safely Ever After

by Maria Fleming
illustrated by Doug Jones

SCHOLASTIC INC.
New York • Toronto • London • Auckland • Sydney
Mexico City • New Delhi • Hong Kong • Buenos Aires

Designed by Maria Lilja
ISBN-13: 978-0-545-08704-9 • ISBN-10: 0-545-08704-X

First printing, October 2008

12 11 10 9 8 7 6 5 4 3 2 1 8 9 10 11 12 13/0

Building Vocabulary With This Book

This book contains eight key words that are important for all children to know. Read the story straight through for enjoyment. Then read it again, pausing to define and discuss each key word. Follow-up the tale with the fun activities on pages 14–16. When you're done, celebrate—kids will have added eight great words to their vocabularies!

Humpty Dumpty sat on a wall.
Humpty Dumpty had a great fall.

KEY WORD: **ignore**

Simple Definition: to pay no attention to something

Sample Sentence: If my little brother starts to poke me, I will just *ignore* him.

A sign told Humpty he shouldn't sit there.
But he chose to **ignore** it—he didn't care!

KEY WORD: **lesson**

Simple Definition: information or a skill you need to learn or study

Sample Sentence: We learned to count to 100 in today's math *lesson*.

Humpty Dumpty learned a **lesson** that day:
Be super safe in every way.

He tells his friends to do the same.
He now knows safety's not a game.

KEY WORD: beware

Simple Definition: to watch out for something that could hurt you

Sample Sentence: *Beware* of dogs you do not know because they may bite.

When you cross the street, take care.
Watch for cars. Be safe. **Beware.**

KEY WORD: **signals**

Simple Definition: bells, whistles, lights, or other signs that tell you what to do

Sample Sentence: My mother stopped the car when the traffic *signal* turned red.

Cross between the crosswalk lines.
Watch the **signals**. Read the signs.

Keep your head safe and sound
when you ride your bike around.

KEY WORD: helmet

Simple Definition: a hard hat that keeps your head safe

Sample Sentence: My brother wears a *helmet* when he plays football, in case he gets hit in the head.

Wear a **helmet**, strap it tight.
Not too big or small—just right!

KEY WORD: **prevent**

Simple Definition: to keep something from happening

Sample Sentence: Brush your teeth to *prevent* cavities.

Don't play with matches. Please be smart.
You can **prevent** fires if you don't let them start.

KEY WORD: **emergency**

Simple Definition: something that happens suddenly and puts someone in danger

Sample Sentence: When there is an *emergency*, the firefighters get on their truck and race down the street.

Emergency! Danger! Whenever there is trouble, call 9-1-1 on the double.

Be a safety star. Do your part.
Learn Humpty's safety tips by heart.

KEY WORD: caution

Simple Definition: doing something very carefully so you don't get hurt

Sample Sentence: Use *caution* when you are near the stove or you might get burned.

Use **caution**, friends, in all you do.
And you'll live safely ever after, too!

Meaning Match

safety words

Listen to the definition. Then go to the WORD CHEST and find a vocabulary word that matches it.

1. to keep something from happening
2. doing something very carefully so you don't get hurt
3. signs that tell you what to do
4. to watch out for something that could hurt you
5. something that happens suddenly and puts someone in danger
6. a hard hat that keeps your head safe
7. to pay no attention to something
8. information or a skill you need to learn or study

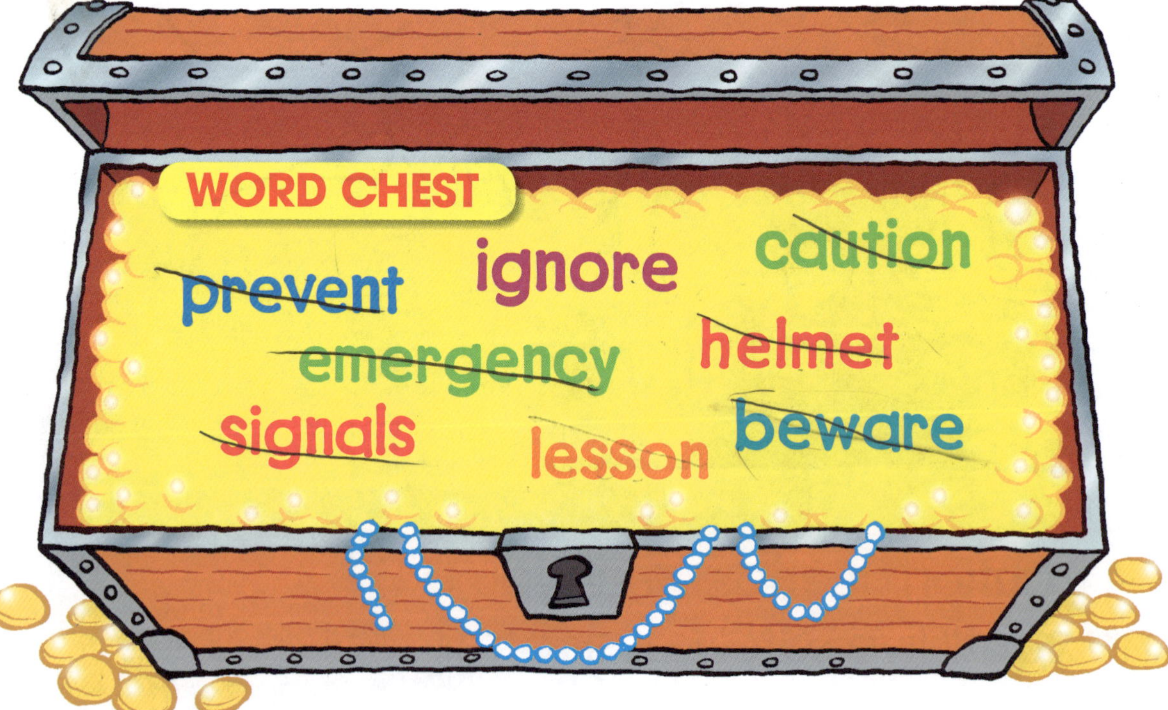

Answers: 1. prevent 2. caution 3. signals 4. beware 5. emergency 6. helmet 7. ignore 8. lesson

Vocabulary Fill-ins

safety words

Listen to the sentence. Then go to the WORD BOX and find the best word to fill in the blank.

WORD BOX

helmet	lesson	beware	emergency
caution	ignore	prevent	signals

1. The crossing guard uses hand ________ to help us cross the street.
2. He has a piano ________ every day.
3. She takes vitamins to help ________ colds.
4. The school nurse came right away when there was an ________ on the playground.
5. I wear a ________ when I in-line skate in case I fall down.
6. My mom uses ________ when she climbs a ladder so that she doesn't fall.
7. When someone is calling for help, you should not ________ it.
8. The three little pigs knew to ________ of the big bad wolf.

Answers: 1. signals 2. lesson 3. prevent 4. emergency 5. helmet 6. caution 7. ignore 8. beware

Vocabulary Questions

safety words

Listen to the question. Think about it. Then answer.

1. Can you think of a time that you learned an important **lesson** about safety? Tell about it.
2. What should you do if there is an **emergency** at home?
3. What dangers should you **beware** of in the kitchen?
4. How should you use **caution** around strangers?
5. What are some things you should **ignore**? What are some things that you should NOT **ignore**?
6. What are some jobs where the workers need to wear **helmets**?
7. How can you help **prevent** yourself from getting hurt on the playground?
8. What **signals** do you sometimes see or hear near train tracks?

Extra: Can you think of some more safety words? Make a list.